The Story of a Special Day
Volume 77

March 17

76th day of the year
(77th in leap years)
289 days remaining
until the end of the year.

by Michael Dobson

Timespinner
Press

Look for other volumes in *The Story of a Special Day*, coming often.

Table of Contents

Cover: Stained glass window of Saint Patrick, for the Event of the Day.

Back Cover: The month of March, from the French Gothic illuminated manuscript *Les Très Riches Heures du duc de Berry.*

March 17 Quotations

"You can't cling to the past. Too many different things are coming into the world."

— Nat King Cole, born March 17, 1919

"The one thing I can guarantee you can expect in life is that you will experience the thoroughly unexpected."

— Dana Reeve, born March 17, 1961

"The future is already here — it's just not very evenly distributed."

— William Gibson, born March 17, 1948

"If you rest, you rust."

— Helen Hayes, died March 17, 1993

"Imitation is the sincerest form of television."

— Fred Allen, died March 17, 1956

"A doctrine is something that pins you down to a given mode of conduct and dozens of situations which you cannot foresee, which is a great mistake in principle."

— George F. Kennan, died March 17, 2005

"Remember that all is opinion."

— Marcus Aurelius, died March 17, 180

"Old men delight in giving good advice as a consolation for the fact that they can no longer provide bad examples."

— François de La Rochefoucauld, died March 17, 1680

Saint Patrick's Day

Saint Patrick (c. 387 — March 17, 493) is known as the Apostle of Ireland. One of the three patron saints of Ireland (although never canonized formally by the Pope), Saint Patrick is by far the best known. His feast day, March 17, is observed both as a religious and as a secular holiday.

The story of Saint Patrick is part historical and part mythical. He was born into a wealthy family in Roman-occupied Britain. At the age of 16, he was kidnapped and taken to Ireland as a slave. He escaped back to Britain, became a priest, and in 432 returned to Ireland as a missionary, where he spent the rest of his life.

In legend, Saint Patrick banished the snakes from Ireland, but it's likely that there were never snakes in the first place. He was supposed to have used the three-leaf shamrock to illustrate the Holy Trinity, but the shamrock had been sacred in pre-Christian Ireland.

While the feast of Saint Patrick was originally a religious observance (it is a Holy Day of Obligation for Catholics in Ireland), by the ninth century it was also being observed as a national day for the Irish.

It was actually blue, not green, that was the original color associated with Saint Patrick. The "wearing of the green" (from the song of the same name) dates to the Irish Rebellion of 1798 *(Éirí Amach)*, an ultimately unsuccessful uprising against British rule. In it, Irish soldiers wore green unforms, and others often wore shamrocks on their clothing.

In 1903, Saint Patrick's Day became an official public holiday in Ireland. Today, the Republic of Ireland uses Saint Patrick's Day to showcase Irish history and culture.

The popularity of Saint Patrick's Day in other countries results from the Irish diaspora that began during the Great Famine of the 1840s. Large number of Irish settled in the United States, Canada, Australia, Argentina, and elsewhere. Today, the descendents of the Irish diaspora number over 100 million, more than 15 times the population of Ireland itself. In all of these countries, Saint Patrick's Day is widely celebrated, and it is often said that on Saint Patrick's Day, everybody's Irish.

In the U.S., Saint Patrick's Day was first

celebrated in colonial times. Many customs are associated with the event. People often wear green, and according to tradition, those who do not are pinched. Green beer is often served. Chicago dyes its river green; Savannah dyes its city fountains green. Because observant Christians are allowed to break their Lenten sacrifices for the day, Saint Patrick's Day is one of the biggest days for alcohol consumption.

The oldest and largest Saint Patrick's Day Parade is held by New York, which began in 1762. It's also the oldest civilian parade in the world. Over 150,000 people march in the parade each year.

Statue of Saint Patrick, Brighton, Massachusetts

March 17 Holidays and Celebrations

Evacuation Day (Massachusetts)

Evacuation Day, celebrated in the Boston area, commemorates the the evacuation of British forces from the city following the Siege of Boston, an event in the American Revolutionary War. The Boston Saint Patrick's Day is officially the Saint Patrick's Day and Evacuation Day Parade, and Revolutionary War reenactors take part in the parade.

British evacuation of Boston

Liberalia (Ancient Rome)

The ancient Roman festival of Liberalia celebrates the Roman god Liber Pater, who was a god of wine, fertility, and freedom. Boys who turned 14 officially became men on that day, discarding their *bulla praetexta* charms and beginning to wear the pure white toga of manhood. To bring fertility to the land, worshippers conducted a processional through the countryside featuring a large phallus.

National Muay Boran Day (Thailand)

The kickboxing method of Muay Thai (มวยไทย), known as the "art of eight weapons," first became popular in the sixteenth century. National Muay Boran Day in Thailand commemorates the legend of Nai Thanomtom, who used muay thai to defeat nine Burmese champions to win his freedom and that of other captives. He was promised a reward of either two wives or great riches. He chose the wives, saying that money was easier to find.

Christian Feast Days

Saints commemorated on March 17 (in addition to Saint Patrick) include Alexius of Rome, Gertrude of Nivelles, and Joseph of Arimathea.

What Happened on March 17?

The abbreviation "O.S." on some dates refers to the fact that the Russian Empire did not switch from the Julian to the Gregorian calendar at the same time as the rest of Europe, and therefore some figures have two dates for their birth or death.

People whose original names are not in the Western alphabet have their native names in the appropriate script shown in parenthesis.

45 BCE - **Caesar's Last Victory**

The Battle of Munda, final battle of the civil war between Julius Caesar and the *boni* faction of the Senate ended with Caesar's victory over the forces of Titus Labienus and Gnaeus Pompeius, allowing him to return to Rome as dictator. His assassination took place on March 15 the following year, leading to the end of the Roman Republic and establishment of the Roman Empire.

1860 CE - **First Taranaki War Begins**

The First Taranaki War, fought between the indigenous Māori people and the British government of New Zealand. Over 3,500 British troops from New Zealand and Australia fought against a Māori force of up to 1,500. The war ended in an inconclusive ceasefire, setting up further land wars between the British settlers and the Māori, which today are fought in courtrooms rather than on the battlefield.

1860 CE - **Kingdom of Italy Proclaimed**

The Italian peninsula was home to numerous small states with a history of internecine war. In the 19th century, a movement for Italian unification began. On March 17, 1860, the newly formed Italian parliament proclaimed a new Kingdom of Italy, a constitutional monarchy headed by Victor Emmanuel II. The kingdom officially lasted through World War II, when a 1946 referendum chose a republican government and abolished the monarchy. The last king, Umberto II, abdicated peacefully and was sent into exile.

Caricature of King Victor Emmanuel II of Italy
by Thomas Nast

1939 CE - **Battle of Nanchang**

In the western world, World War II is considered to have started with Germany's invasion of Poland on September 1, 1939. However, the Japan had already been at war with China since July 7, 1937. On March 17, 1939, the Japanese, who had already taken Beijing and Wuhan turned to the next target: the strategic railway center of Nanchang. Some 120,000 Japanese troops battled over 200,000 Chinese, but the Chinese forces lacked vehicles. The battle lasted nearly two months, ending in Japanese victory.

1941 CE - **National Gallery of Art Opens**

On March 17, 1941, President Franklin Delano Roosevelt inaugurated the National Gallery of Art. At the time of its opening, it was the largest marble structure in the world. The site on which it was built had been the railroad station where President James Garfield was assassinated in 1881. Financier Andrew Mellon provided funding, and his private collection formed the basis of the new museum. Today, the National Gallery of Art is home to paintings by Rembrandt, Leonardo da Vinci, El Greco, and many others.

1942 CE - **Bełżec Extermination Camp Opens**

Originally, Nazi concentration camps were prisons providing forced labor, but as the war continued, the camps became ever more brutal. In 1942, the Nazi government decided to undertake the "Final Solution," in which the Jews in Europe would be liquidated altogether. Bełżec, the first camp designed solely for mass killing, began operation on March 17, 1942. Although Bełżec alone accounted for at least 400,000 Holocaust victims, it is little known today because there were very few survivors.

Memorial at Bełżec

1945 CE - **The Ludendorff Bridge Collapses**

The Ludendorff Bridge was made famous in the 1969 film *The Bridge at Remagen.* On March 7-8, 1945, advancing Allied troops were surprised to discover the bridge was still standing and captured it, allowing rapid movement of forces across the Rhine River into Germany. On March 17, eleven V-2 rockets were fired at the bridge, weaking it so that it suddenly collapsed into the Rhine. By then, however, the American forces had established a bridgehead on the German side and built a pontoon bridge.

The Ludendorff Bridge after collapse

1950 CE - **Californium Revealed**

Californium (Cf), an artificial element with atomic number 98, was first synthesized in a cyclotron at the University of California, Berkeley. About 5,000 atoms were produced, with a half-life of 44 minutes. On March 17, 1950, researchers announced their findings, naming the new element after the university where it was first made. Californium is used as a neutron startup source in some nuclear reactors, provides treatment for certain cervical and brain cancers, and is used in portable metal detectors and other detection devices.

1964 CE - **Vanguard 1 Launched**

Vanguard 1 was the second artificial satellite placed in orbit by the United Sates, the fourth overall, and the first solar-powered satellite. It provided a test of a three-stage rocket and provided many useful measurements. It operated for nearly seven years, but with a lifetime of 240 years, it is now the oldest man-made object still in Earth orbit, circling the globe every two hours and 14 minutes.

1959 CE - **The Dalai Lama Departs Tibet**

The Tibetan uprising of 1959 began with a revolt in the Tibetan capital of Lhasa on March 10. Fearing a possible Chinese abduction,the Dalai Lama, who was both the religious and secular head of the Tibetan government, decided to flee the country for neighboring India, leaving on the night of March 17, 1959, disguised as a soldier. He and his party crossed into India on March 31, where he was subsequently granted asylum, establishing the Tibetan government in exile. The Dalai Lama won the Nobel Peace Prize in 1989.

1966 CE - **DSV *Alvin* Retrieves a Hydrogen Bomb**

In January 1966, a B-52 bomber collided with a tanker over the Mediterranean Sea, killing several people on both airplanes, and losing four hydrogen bombs in the process. Three H-bombs were recovered on land, but the fourth fell into the sea. The last bomb was recovered by the first Deep Submergence Vehicle (DSV), *Alvin,* who retrieved it from a depth of nearly 3,000 feet. The DSV *Alvin* went on to other feats, including the exploration of the wreckage of RMS *Titanic* in 1986.

DSV *Alvin*

1969 CE - **Golda Meir Becomes Prime Minister of Israel**

Golda Meir, previously foreign minister, was elected as prime minister of Israel on March 17, 1969. She was the first woman to hold the office in Israel, and the third woman in the world to be an elected head of state. She was called the "Iron Lady" long before Margaret Thatcher was associated with the term.

Golda Meir

1988 CE - **Battle of Afabet**

The Eritrean War for Independence, which began in 1961 and lasted until 1991, achieved a major turning point on March 17-20, 1988, at the Battle of Afabet, a major loss for Ethiopia, which sought to keep Eritrea as part of the country. Eritrea achieved independence following a referendum in 1993.

1992 CE - **South Africa Votes on Apartheid**

On March 17, 1992, in a referendum restricted to white voters, 68% of the South African electorate voted to support the ending of the apartheid system in that country.

Who Was Born on March 17?

Acting

Julia Winter (March 17, 1993 —)

Julia Winter played Veruca Salt in the 2005 remake of *Charlie and the Chocolate Factory*.

Eliza Bennett (March 17, 1992 —)

English actress Eliza Bennett appeared in *Nanny McPhee, Inkheart, The Contractor,* and *From Time to Time.*

Rob Kardashian (March 17, 1987 —)

Kardashian appeared on his family's reality shows *Keeping Up With the Kardashians* and *Khloé & Lamar*, as well as on *Dancing with the Stars*.

Oleysa Rulin (Олеся Рулин) (March 17, 1986 —)

Russian-American actress Oleysa Rulin appeared in the first three *High School Musical* films as Kelsi.

Coco Austin (March 17, 1979 —)

Actress and glamour model Coco Austin has appeared in numerous swimsuit and lingerie catalogues, in Playboy® magazine, and in films and TV shows. She married rapper Ice-T in 2001.

Brittany and Cynthia Daniel (March 17, 1976 —)

The Daniel twins are best known for playing the Wakefield sisters on the teen drama *Sweet Valley High*.

Natalie Zea (March 17, 1975 —)

Zea appeared as Gwen on the soap opera *Passions*, Karen on *Dirty Sexy Money*, and Winona on *Justified.*

Puneeth Rajkumar (March 17, 1975 —)

Bollywood star Rajkumar won the National Film Award for Best Child Artist in 1986, and achieved a record of 18 films in a row that stayed in theaters for a minimum of 100 days. He hosts the quiz show *Kannadada Kotyadhipati*, modeled on *Who Wants to Be a Millionaire?*

Gina Holden (March 17, 1975 —)

Holden was Coreen on *Blood Ties*, Dale Arden in the 2007 *Flash Gordon* TV series, and Shea on *Harper's Island*.

Marisa Coughlan (March 17, 1974 —)

Coughlan began in 1999's *Teaching Mrs. Tingle* and appeared in the TV series *Boston Legal*.

Amelia Heinle (March 17, 1973 —)

Heinle appeared in the soap operas *Loving, All My Children*, and *The Young and the Restless*. She was nominated for "Outstanding Female Newcomer" in the *Soap Opera Digest* Awards.

Yanic Truesdale (March 17, 1970 —)

Truesdale played Michel in the TV series *Gilmore Girls*.

Matthew St. Patrick (March 17, 1968 —)

St. Patrick played Keith in *Six Feet Under,* Detective Taggert on *General Hospital*, and Adrian on *All My Children*.

Jeremy Sheffield (March 17, 1966 —)

English actor Sheffield appeared in the BBCOne series *Holby City* and the ITV series *Murder in Suburbia*, and in the film *The Wedding Date*.

Rob Lowe (March 17, 1964 —)

Rob Lowe was a prominent member of the Brat Pack of actors, appearing in such films as *About Last Night...* and *St. Elmo's Fire*. As a TV actor, he appeared in *The West Wing* and *Parks and Recreation*.

Rob Lowe

Clare Grogan (March 17, 1970 —)

Scottish actress Grogan appeared in *Gregory's Girl*, the BBC series *Blott on the Landscape* and *Red Dwarf*, and in *EastEnders*.

Casey Siemaszko (March 17, 1961 —)

Siemaszko appeared in two *Back to the Future* films, *Stand by Me*, *Young Guns*, and TV series including *St. Elsewhere*, *The Facts of Life*, and the *Law & Order* franchise.

Andrew Paul (March 17, 1961 —)

British actor Paul played PC Dave Quinnan in *The Bill* for 13 years.

Vicki Lewis (March 17, 1960 —)

Lewis played Beth in the NBC sitcom *NewsRadio*.

Arye Gross (March 17, 1960 —)

Gross played Adam in the TV series *Ellen*, co-starred in *Citizen Baines*, and played the medical examiner in *Castle*.

Rebecca Arthur (March 17, 1960 —)

Arthur is best known as Mary Anne Spencer on the TV series *Perfect Strangers*.

Christian Clemenson (March 17, 1958 —)

Clemenson won an Emmy for playing Jerry "Hands" Espenson in the TV series *Boston Legal*.

Rory McGrath (March 17, 1956 —)

English comedian McGrath appeared in *Who Dares Wins, Chelmsford 123, Three Men in a Boat*, and as a panelist on *They Think It's All Over.*

Gary Sinese (March 17, 1955 —)

Gary Sinese was nominated for an Academy Award for his role in *Forrest Gump*, won a Golden Globe for the title role in *Truman*, and an Emmy for the title role in the TV film *Wallace*. He has also starred in the TV series *CSI:NY*.

Gary Sinese

Mark Boone Junior (March 17, 1955 —)

Boone played Bobby in the FX series *Sons of Anarchy* and appeared in the Christopher Nolan films *Memento* and *Batman Begins*.

Lesley-Anne Down (March 17, 1954 —)

Down played in *Upstairs, Downstairs*, *The Pink Panther Strikes Again*, the miniseries *North and South* (receiving a Golden Globe nomination), *Dallas*, *Sunset Beach*, and *The Bold and the Beautiful*.

Kurt Russell (March 17, 1951 —)

Russell was a top star for Walt Disney pictures in the 1970s. He was nominated for an Emmy for playing Elvis and a Golden Globe for his work opposite Meryl Streep in *Silkwood*. He is known for his role as Snake in the John Carpenter films *Escape from New York* and its sequel *Escape from L.A.*

Patrick Duffy (March 17, 1949 —)

Duffy is best known as Bobby Ewing in the long-running CBS prime time soap opera *Dallas*.

Rudy Ray Moore (March 17, 1927 — October 19, 2008)

Moore was best known as "Dolemite" from the 1975 film of the same name and its sequels *The Human Tornado* and *The Return of Dolemite*.

Brigitte Helm (March 17, 1906 — June 11, 1996)

Helm played Maria and her robotic double in Fritz Lang's classic 1927 silent film *Metropolis*.

Brigitte Helm

Art

Patrick McDonnell (March 17, 1956 —)

McDonnell created the syndicated daily comic strip *Mutts* and the monthly *Bad Baby* for *Parent's Magazine*.

Henry Bumstead (March 17, 1915 — May 24, 2006)

Art director and production designer Henry Bumstead won Academy Awards for *To Kill a Mockingbird* and *The Sting*, and was nominated for *Vertigo* and *Unforgiven*.

Kate Greenaway (March 17, 1846 — November 6, 1901)

English children's book author and illustrator Kate Greenaway inspired a generation of children's clothes in the 1880s and 1890s. The Kate Greenaway Medal in children's book illustration is awarded in her honor.

Polly from *The Queen of the Pirate Isle*, illustration by Kate Greenaway

Crime

Barry Minkow (March 17, 1962 —)

Minkow's carpet cleaning company was actually a front for a Ponzi scheme that cost inventors $100 million. Following his prison term, he became a pastor and fraud investigator, but was incarcerated again after attempting to manipulate the stock price of homebuilder Lennar.

John Wayne Gacy (March 17, 1942 — May 10, 1994)

Serial killer and rapist Gacy murdered at least 33 teenage boys between 1972 and 1978, and was executed in May 1994.

Dance

Rudolf Nureyev (Рудо́льф Нуре́ев) (March 17, 1938 — January 6, 1993)

One of the most celebrated ballet dancers of the 20th century, Nureyev defected from the Soviet Union in 1961. He is credited for changing the perception of male ballet dancers and for crossing the borders between classical ballet and modern dance.

Rudolf Nureyev

Fashion

Alexander McQueen (March 17, 1969 — February 11, 2010)

British fashion designer Alexander McQueen was chief designer of Givenchy before founding a label under his own name. He won four British Designer of the Year Awards and the International Designer of the Year Award.

Journalism

Jorge Ramos (March 17, 1958 —)

Ramos won eight Emmys as the anchorman for Univision News, and wrote the best-selling *No Borders: A Journalist's Search for Home*.

Michael Kelly (March 17, 1957 — April 3, 2003)

Journalist Kelly worked for The Washington *Post*, the New York *Times*, *The New Yorker, The New Republic*, and *The Atlantic*. He was the first U.S. journalist to be killed in Iraq.

Music

Melissa Auf der Maur (March 17, 1972 —)

Auf der Maur played bass with the alternative rock band Hole and subsequently played with The Smashing Pumpkins and embarked on her own solo career.

Gene Ween (March 17, 1970 —)

Aaron Freeman was a founding member of the experimental alternative rock group Ween under his stage name.

Billy Corgan (March 17, 1967 —)

Corgan is the front man and sole permanent member of The Smashing Pumpkins.

Paul Overstreet (March 17, 1955 —)

Country singer Overstreet has topped the *Billboard* country charts twice, won two Grammys and two Song of the Year Awards, and was named BMI Songwriter of the Year for an unprecedented five straight years.

Susie Allanson (March 17, 1952 —)

Country singer Allanson was named "Best New Female Singer" in 1979 by *Billboard* Magazine and won the Country Radio Broadcaster's "New Faces of Country Music" award the same year. She had a #2 hit with "We Belong Together."

Scott Gorham (March 17, 1951 —)

Gorham was one of the "twin lead guitarists" of the Irish rock band Thin Lizzy.

John Sebastian (March 17, 1944 —)

Founding member of The Lovin' Spoonful, Sebastian's (below) hits include "Do You Believe in Magic," "Summer in the City," and "Did You Ever Have to Make Up Your Mind?" He is a member of the Rock and Roll Hall of Fame.

Paul Kantner (March 17, 1941 —)

Rocker Kantner co-founded Jefferson Airplane and its spin-off Jefferson Starship.

Nat King Cole (March 17, 1919 — February 15, 1965)

Nat King Cole's (below) hits include "Mona Lisa," "Unforgettable," and "Those Lazy-Hazy-Crazy Days of Summer." He was the first African-American to host a TV variety show.

Ray Ellington (March 17, 1915 — February 27, 1985)

Singer and drummer Ellington is best known for his appearances on the British radio comedy program *The Goon Show* from 1951 to 1960.

Alfred Newman (March 17, 1901 — February 17, 1970)

Newman composed the music for over 200 films including *The King and I, Camelot,* and *State Fair*. He won nine Academy Awards in 45 nominations.

Newsmakers

Dana Reeve (March 17, 1961 — March 6, 2006)

Singer, actress and disability advocate Dana Reeve is best known as the widow of actor Christopher Reeve, who became paralyzed following a riding accident. She died in 2005 of lung cancer, although she had never smoked cigarettes.

Barry Horne (March 17, 1952 — November 5, 2001)

English animal rights activist Barry Horne became known for his 68-day hunger strike about animal testing, received an 18-year sentence for planting incendiary devices in stores selling fur and leather products, and died on the fifteenth day of another hunger strike in 2001.

Pattie Boyd (March 17, 1944 —)

Model and photographer Pattie Boyd was married to George Harrison and Eric Clapton, and claims to be the inspiration for such songs as "Something," "For You Blue," and "Layla." She had a small part in the Beatles film *A Hard Day's Night*, where she met Harrison.

Pattie Boyd (right) with George Harrison
in *A Hard Day's Night*

Robin Knox-Johnston (March 17, 1939 —)

Sailor Knox-Johnston was the first man to perform a single-handed non-stop circumnavigation of the glove by sailboat and won the Jules Verne Trophy for a subsequent record-setting circumnavigation with co-skipper Peter Blake.

Lawrence "Titus" Oates (March 17, 1880 — March 16 or 17, 1912)

The British Antarctic Expedition, also known as the Terra Nova Expedition, was an attempt to be first to reach the South Pole, but were beaten by Roald Amundsen. On the return journey, expedition member Lawrence "Titus" Oates became ill. Rather than burden his teammates, on March 16, 1912, he stepped out of the tent to die, saying "I am just going outside and I may be some time." His sacrifice was in vain; the rest of the team died before the month was out. Search parties later recovered journals, photos, and bodies, revealing the story of Oates's sacrifice.

Terra Nova Expedition at the South Pole

(standing, from left to right) Edward Wilson, Robert Falcon Scott (leader), *Lawrence Oates*

(sitting, left to right) Henry Bowers, and Lt."Teddy" Evans

Jim Bridger (March 17, 1804 — July 17, 1881)

Bridger was one of the foremost mountain men of the early West. He was one of the first European-Americans to see the geysers of Yellowstone, the Great Salt Lake, and other natural wonders.

Politics and Military

Cynthia McKinney (March 17, 1955 —)

Six-term congresswoman McKinney was the first African-American woman to represent Georgia in the House of Representatives and ran as the Green Party candidate for President in 2008.

Michael Hayden (March 17, 1945 —)

Four-star USAF general Hayden was director of the National Security Agency and the Central Intelligence Agency.

Myrlie Evers-Williams (March 17, 1933 —)

Civil rights activist Evers-Williams was the wife of murdered activist Medgard Evers in 1963. She worked for 33 years to bring her husband's murderer to justice and became chairwoman of the NAACP.

Meir Amit (מאיר עמית) (March 17, 1921 — July 17, 2009)

Amit was Chief Director of Mossad, and is considered the most successful intelligence officer in Israeli history.

Sheikh Mujibur Rahman (March 17, 1920 — August 15, 1975)

Sheikh Mujib was the founder of Bangladesh, and served as its first president and later as prime minister.

Bayard Rustin (March 17, 1912 — August 24, 1987)

Leading early civil rights activist Rustin initiated a 1947 Freedom Ride to challenge segregation on interstate busing, and was an early advocate of Gandhi's nonviolent resistance strategy. He was chief organizer of the 1963 March on Washington and was an early leader in the gay rights movement.

Bayard Rustin

Pierce Butler (March 17, 1866 — November 16, 1939)

Butler was associate justice of the U.S. Supreme Court from 1923 until his death.

Roger B. Taney (March 17, 1777 — October 12, 1864)

Taney was the fifth Chief Justice of the U.S. Supreme Court, serving from 1836 until his death. He is best known for the *Dred Scott* decision that removed restrictions on the spread of slavery, which is considered one of the indirect causes of the Civil War.

Lachlan McIntosh (March 17, 1725 — February 20, 1906)

A military leader during the American Revolution, McIntosh is known for his 1777 duel in which he shot and killed Button Gwinnett, a signer of the Declaration of Independence.

James IV of Scotland (March 17, 1473 — September 9, 1513)

King James IV of Scotland's war with Henry VIII of England ended with his disastrous defeat at the Battle of Flodden Field, in which he became the last monarch from anywhere in Great Britain to be killed in battle.

Science, Engineering, and Space

Ken Mattingly (March 17, 1936 —)

Astronaut Ken Mattingly flew on the Apollo 16 mission and commanded two Space Shuttle flights.

David Peakall (March 17, 1931 — August 18, 2001)

Toxicologist David Peakall's research on the effects of DDT led to the chemical's banning in the United States.

James Irwin (March 17, 1930 — August 8, 1991)

Astronaut James Irwin (right) was the Lunar Module pilot for Apollo 15 and the eighth person to walk on the Moon. Following his NASA career, he led expeditions to Mount Ararat in search of the remains of Noah's Ark. He died of a heart attack in 1991.

Charles F. Brush (March 17, 1849 — June 15, 1929)

Inventor and entrepreneur Brush is known for designing the dynamo to power arc lights. He also designed the first wind turbine. He won the Edison Medal, the Rumford Prize, the French Legion of Honor, and the Franklin Medal for his achievements.

Gottlieb Daimler (March 17, 1834 — March 6, 1900)

Automobile pioneer Gottlieb Daimler invented the high-speed petrol engine and the first four-wheel automobile. His company Daimler Motors was merged with Karl Benz's company to form Daimler AG, manufacturers of Mercedes-Benz automobiles.

Sports

Aaron Baddeley (March 17, 1981 —)

American-born Australian golfer Baddeley won the PGA Tour of Australasia Order of Merit and has been listed in the top twenty ranking of golfers in the world.

Samoa Joe (March 17, 1979 —)

Wrestler Nuufoulau Joel Seanoa has won the Ring of Honor World Championship and the TNA World Heavyweight Championship.

Test (March 17, 1975 — March 13, 2009)

Wrestler Andrew Martin worked for WWF/WWE and TNA, winning six championships. He died of an accidental overdose while dealing with chronic traumatic encephalopathy, an Alzheimer's-like condition caused by repeated concussions and head injuries.

Mia Hamm (March 17, 1972 —)

Mia Hamm scored 158 international goals, more than any other player, male or female, in the history of soccer. She was named FIFA World Player of the Year twice and inducted into the National Soccer Hall of Fame.

Edgar Grospiron (March 17, 1969 —)

French freestyle skier Grospiron won the gold medal at the 1992 Winter Olympics in moguls, and a bronze medal at the 1994 Olympics.

Chuck Muncie (March 17, 1953 —)

Running back Muncie tied the NFL season record for rushing touchdowns in 1981, appeared on the cover of *Sports Illustrated* twice, and served 18 months for cocaine distribution.

Sammy Baugh (March 17, 1914 — December 17, 2008)

Washington Redskin "Slingin' Sammy" Baugh was inducted into the College Football Hall of Fame in 1951 and the Pro Football Hall of Fame in 1963.

Sonny Werblin (March 17, 1910 — November 21, 1991)

Sports impresario Werblin owned the New York Jets, chaired Madison Square Garden, and built the Meadowlands Sports Complex.

Bobby Jones (March 17, 1902 — December 18, 1971)

Jones was the most successful amateur golfer to compete on a national and international level. He is a member of the World Golf Hall of Fame.

Ralph Rose (March 17, 1885 — October 16, 1913)

Rose won three gold, two silver, and one bronze Olympic medal in track and field events for the United States in the 1904, 1908, and 1912 Olympic Games. He died at the age of 28 from typhoid fever.

Ralph Rose

Writing

William Gibson (March 17, 1948 —)

Science fiction writer William Gibson is known as a pioneer of the "cyberpunk" movement with his 1984 novel Neuromancer. He coined the term "cyberspace." Gibson has won every important award in science fiction, including the Hugo and Nebula Awards, is a member of the Science Fiction Hall of Fame, and is credited as an inspiration for the 1999 film *The Matrix*.

James Morrow (March 17, 1947 —)

Science fiction and fantasy author Morrow is known for the Godhead Trilogy, which won the World Fantasy Award in 1995.

Paul Green (March 17, 1894 — May 4, 1981)

Green received the Pulitzer Prize for his 1927 play *In Abraham's Bosom*.

Who Died on March 17?

Acting and Film

Michael Gough (November 23, 1916 — March 17, 2011)

Gough appeared in Hammer horror films in the 1950s and 1960s, and is best known for playing Alfred the butler in the four Burton/Schumacher *Batman* films between 1989 and 1997.

Rosetta LeNoire (August 8, 1911 — March 17, 2002)

LeNoire was the goddaughter of Bill "Bojangles" Robinson, and began her career in the 1939 version of The *Hot Mikado*. She is best known for her roles on *Gimme a Break!, Amen*, and as Estelle on *Family Matters*. She received the National Medal of Arts in 1999 for her contributions to diversity in theatrical casting.

René Clément (March 18, 1913 — March 17, 1996)

Director René Clément won two Academy Awards for Best Foreign Language Film for 1950's *Au-delà des grilles* and 1952's *Jeux interdits.*

Mai Zetterling (May 24, 1925 — March 17, 1994)

Zetterling starred in a number of English films with such actors of Tyrone Power, Richard Widmark, Peter Sellars, and Richard Attenborough, and became a noted Swedish director starting with her 1964 film *Älskande par,* which critic Kenneth Tynan called "one of the most ambitious debuts since *Citizen Kane.*"

Helen Hayes (October 10, 1900 — March 17, 2003)

Known as the "First Lady of the American Theater," Helen Hayes is one of only eleven people who have won an Emmy, a Grammy, a Oscar, and a Tony Award. She received the National Medal of Arts in 1988 and the Helen Hayes Awards for professional theatre in the greater Washington, DC, area are named for her.

Helen Hayes

Grace Stafford (November 7, 1903 — March 17, 1992)

Gracie Boyle Lanz, wife of animation producer Walter Lanz, is best known under her stage name as the voice of Woody Woodpecker.

Capucine (January 6, 1928 — March 17, 1990)

Model and actress Capucine (Germaine Hélène Irène Lefebvre) is best known for her roles in *The Pink Panther* and *What's New Pussycat?* She committed suicide in 1990 by jumping from her 8th floor apartment in Switzerland.

Merritt Butrick (September 3, 1959 — March 17, 1989)

Buttrick was known for playing the son of Captain James T. Kirk in the films *Star Trek II: The Wrath of Khan* and its sequel *Star Trek III: The Search for Spock.*

Fred Allen (May 31, 1894 — March 17, 1956)

One of the best-known humorists of the Golden Age of American Radio, Fred Allen was known for his long running fake feud with Jack Benny and for his comic creation "Allen's Alley."

Architecture

Louis Kahn (February 20, 1901 — March 17, 1974)

American architect Louis Kahn is considered one of the most influential architects of the 20th century. His famous works include the Yale University Art Gallery, the Salk Institute, the Bangladesh National Assembly Building, the First Unitarian Church of Rochester, New York, and many others.

Courtyard of the Salk Institute for Biological Studies,
designed by Louis Kahn

Business

Pat Weaver (December 21, 1908 — March 17, 2002)

Radio executive Pat Weaver became president of NBC in 1953, and is credited with establishing the format of commercial broadcasting in the transition from radio to television as the dominant medium. His daughter is actress Sigourney Weaver.

Crime

Ronnie Kray (October 24, 1933 — March 17, 1995)

The Kray twins, Ronnie and Reggie, were major organized crime figures in London's East End during the 1950s and 1960s. They were involved in armed robberies, protection rackets, and several murders. Their public identity as nightclub owners brought them into contact with prominent entertainers, including Frank Sinatra and Judy Garland, as well as with politicians. They were arrested in 1968 and sentenced to life imprisonment.

Santo Trafficante, Jr. (November 15, 1914 — March 17, 1987)

Trafficante led organized crime in Florida and Cuba, where he was reputedly the most important Mafioso in Batista-era Cuba. He was allied with various organized crime outfits in New York and Chicago. He was never convicted of a crime.

Juraj Jánošík (baptized January 25, 1688 — March 17, 1713)

Slovakian highwayman Jánošík became the Robin Hood of Slovak legend, famed for robbing nobles and giving to the poor. He was arrested and hanged in 1713, but his story has become a symbol of resistance to oppression. A number of poems and films portray his modern legend.

Juraj Jánošík

Fashion

Oleg Cassini (April 11, 1913 — March 17, 2006)

Fashion designer Oleg Cassini is best known for "The Jackie Look," his designs for First Lady Jacqueline Kennedy. He also costumed numerous films and worked with movie stars ranging from Rita Hayworth to Marilyn Monroe.

Music

Ferlin Husky (December 3, 1925 — March 17, 2011)

Country music singer Ferlin Husky had two dozen Top 20 Billboard hits between 1953 and 1975, including "Gone" and "Wings of a Dove." He is a member of the Country Music Hall of Fame.

Alex Chilton (December 28, 1950 — March 17, 2010)

Chilton was the lead singer of the Box Tops, best known for his 1967 hit "The Letter."

Ernest Gold (July 13, 1921 — March 17, 1999)

Motion picture composer Ernest Gold wrote scores for such films as *Exodus, It's a Mad Mad Mad Mad World*, and *On the Beach*, receiving four Academy Award and three Golden Globe nominations, winning the Oscar for *Exodus*.

Jermaine Stewart (September 7, 1957 — March 17, 1997)

Stewart is best known for his 1986 hit "We Don't Have to Take Our Clothes Off."

Terry Stafford (November 22, 1941 — March 17, 1996)

Stafford is best known for his 1964 Top Ten hit "Suspicion" and his 1973 country hit "Amarillo by Morning."

Politics and Military

John Demjanjuk (Іван Дем'янюк) (April 3, 1920 — March 17, 2012)

Ukrainian-American auto worker Demjanjuk was first convicted of being "Ivan the Terrible," a concentration camp guard at Treblinka, but his conviction was overturned after evidence showed "Ivan the Terrible" was most likely another man. He was charged again for being a guard at the Sobibór and Majdanek camps and convicted again, but died while the verdict was on appeal.

George F. Kennan (February 16, 1904 — March 17, 2005)

Kennan was Ambassador to the Soviet Union in the early 1950s and is considered a key figure in the strategy of containment of the Cold War. He was involved in the implementation of the Marshall Plan and helped formulate the Truman Doctrine.

Pat Clayton (April 16, 1896 — March 17, 1962)

British surveyor and soldier Clayton was the basis for the character of Peter Madox in *The English Patient*.

Susanna M. Salter (March 2, 1860 — March 17, 1961)

Former Mayor of Argonia, Kansas, Salter was the first woman elected to any political office in the United States.

Marcus Aurelius (April 26, 121 — March 17, 180)

Marcus Aurelius was the 16th emperor of Rome as well as an important Stoic philosopher. Considered a "philosopher king," his book *Meditations* is still read today.

Marcus Aurelius

Science

John Backus (December 3, 1924 — March 17, 2007)

Backus invented the high-level programming language FORTRAN and of the Backus-Naur form (BNF) notation. He received the National Medal of Science and the ACM Turing Award for his work.

Irène Joliot-Curie (September 12, 1897 — March 17, 1956)

Joliot-Curie (right) was the daughter of famed scientists Marie Skłodowska-Curie and Pierre Curie. She shared the 1935 Nobel Prize in Chemistry with her husband Frédéric Joliot-Curie for the discovery of artificial radioactivity.

Christian Doppler (November 29, 1803 — March 17, 1853)

Mathematician and physicist Christian Doppler developed the principle that the observed frequency of a wave depends on the relative speed of source and observer, which is known as the *Doppler effect*. The Doppler effect explains why the sound of a siren changes pitch as the emergency vehicle comes closer or farther away, and also helps determine the speed of distant stars and galaxies relative to our solar system.

Daniel Bernoulli (February 8, 1700 — March 17, 1782)

Daniel Bernoulli was only one of the many mathematicians in the talented Bernoulli family. He did pioneering work in probability, statistics, and fluid mechanics. *Bernoulli's principle* describes the relationship between the speed of a fluid and changes in its pressure. Applications of the principle include the carburetor, the Pitot tube, and the Dyson Bladeless Fan.

Sports

Ray Meyer (December 18, 1913 — March 17, 2006)

DePaul University basketball coach Ray Meyer

led his team to 21 post-season appearances from 1942 to 1984. He is a member of the Naismith Memorial Basketball Hall of Fame.

Amos Alonzo Stagg (August 16, 1862 — March 17, 1965)

Legendary football coach Amos Alonzo Stagg was active in other sports as well. He was the first person to be inducted into the College Football Hall of Fame as both a player and a coach, and was also inducted into the Basketball Hall of Fame. His football contributions include developing the 7-2-2 defense, the tackling dummy, the Statue of Liberty Play, and varsity letters.

Writing

Andre Norton (February 17, 1912 — March 17, 2005)

Under her pen names Andre Norton, Andrew North, and Allen Weston, science fiction and fantasy author Alice Mary Norton was the first woman to win the Gandalf Grand Master Award for fantasy and the Damon Knight Memorial Grand Master Award for science fiction. She was published over 300 times in her prolific career.

François de La Rochefoucauld
(September 15, 1613 — March 17, 1680)

French author La Rochefoucauld (below) was known for his memoirs and for his many maxims.

March: The Third Month

In ancient Rome, March was the first month of the year. As the first month of spring, in the Mediterranean climate it marked the beginning of the military campaign season. That's why March (Martius) is named in honor of Mars, the Roman god of war.

Although the first month of the year was moved back to January sometime during the transition of Rome from a kingdom to a republic (historians differ), March was the first month of the year in Russia until the end of the 15th Century, and is the first month of the year in many other cultures and religions.

In the northern hemisphere, March 1 marks the beginning of meteorological spring. In the southern hemisphere, March is the equivalent of September, making southern hemisphere March the beginning of autumn.

March is one of the seven months that have 31 days in it. March starts on the same day of the week as November every year, and except for leap years starts on the same day as February. March starts on the same day of the week as the previous June except for leap years, and in leap years starts on the same day as the previous September and December.

March in Other Cultures

In Finland, March is called *maaliskuu* (earthy month). In Ukraine, it's *березень* (birch tree). Other names for March include *Lentmonat* (Saxon), *Hyld-monath* (Angles), and *sušec* (Slovene).

March Symbols

Birthstones:
Aquamarine and bloodstone, both representing courage.

Aquamarine

Birth Flowers: Daffodils

Daffodils in Bagatelle Park, Paris, France

March Events

Honorary months: Presidents, Congresses, and nations around the world issue proclamations recognizing particular months to honor certain causes. These events generally fall in March. (All US unless otherwise noted.)

- National Nutrition Month
- American Red Cross Month
- Women's History Month (celebrated in Canada during October)

- Irish-American Heritage Month
- Colorectal Cancer Awareness Month
- Fire Prevention Month (The Philippines)

"March Madness": (United States) The NCAA Men's Division I Basketball Championship, popularly known as "March Madness" or the "Big Dance," is a single-elimination tournament to establish the champion college basketball team.

Multi-day events: Some March events span multiple days.

- **Nineteen Day Fast:** (Bahá'í Faith) March 2 through March 20

- **Girl Scout Week:** (U.S.) The week that includes March 12, the date of the founding of the first chapter of the Girl Scouts of the USA in 1912. The earliest Girl Scout Week can start is March 6, and the latest it can end is March 18. The Sunday of Girl Scout Week is celebrated by some churches as Girl Scout Sunday or Girl Scout Sabbath.

- **Multiple Sclerosis Awareness Week:** (U.S.) Sponsored by the National Multiple Sclerosis Society, MS Awareness Week is normally held on the second full week in March. The earliest it can begin is March 9 and the latest it can end is March 21.

Movable events: Some events change dates from year to year.

- **Passion Sunday:** The fifth Sunday of the Christian season of Lent is known as Passion Sunday in various Protestant denominations and by some traditionalist Catholics. Sometimes, the sixth Sunday of Lent is referred to as Passion Sunday, but it is more commonly known as Palm Sunday. Passion Sunday starts the two week Passiontide, which ends on Holy Saturday, the day before Easter, commemorating the day that Jesus's body was laid in the tomb. The fifth Sunday of Lent can occur as early as March 8 (though the next time it will be that early is in 2285 CE), and as late as April 11.

- **Palm Sunday:** The moveable feast of Palm Sunday commemorates the triumphant entry of Jesus into Jerusalem, an event mentioned in all four gospels. In many Christian churches, palm leaves are distributed to the worshippers. The earliest date for Palm Sunday is March 15, and the latest is April 18.

March Zodiac Signs

From the perspective of someone on Earth, the Sun appears to move through the sky throughout the year, along a path astronomers call the ecliptic plane. The ecliptic plane is divided into twelve constellations, known as the zodiac, based on traditionally observed patterns of stars. On your birthday, you can't see your constellation, because it's part of the daytime sky.

The zodiac was first developed by Babylonian astronomers about 2,500 years ago. Because they were unaware that the Earth wobbles like a spinning top (a motion known as *precession*), they didn't make allowance for the fact that the Sun's path through the zodiac changes over time.

That means there are now two sets of dates for your birth sign. The tropical dates are the original Babylonian dates; the siderial dates tell you where the Sun actually appears as it moves along its annual path.

March 17 is one of the few days that has the same astrological sign in both systems: Pisces.

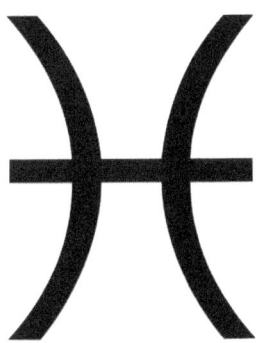

Pisces

Tropical February 20 to March 20

Siderial March 15 to April 14

In the Roman legend of Venus and her son Cupid, they escaped the clutches of Typhon, known as the "father of all monsters," by transforming into fish and tying themselves together with rope. That's why the name Pisces is plural for fish. The constellation appears as a somewhat ragged "V" shape, representing the rope, with the "fish" located at the two rope ends.

In astrology, Pisces is a water sign, compatible with the other water signs Cancer and Scorpio, as well as with the earth signs Taurus, Virgo, and Capricorn. Pisceans are supposed to be imaginative, compassionate, unworldly, secretive, and escapist.

What Day of the Week is March 17?

On what day of the week does March 17 fall?

Surprisingly, this isn't an easy question. Because the calendar year is 365 days long (366 in leap years), it doesn't divide evenly by the seven days of the week.

Also, the Earth goes around the Sun in about 365-1/4 days, so a calendar tends to drift over time. That's why the same date falls on different weekdays in different years.

This is made even more complicated by a change in calendars that took place in 1582. Our modern calendar has its roots in ancient Rome, in a calendar reform conducted by Julius Caesar. Caesar commissioned mathematicians to attack the problem, and came up with the idea of *leap years,* and thus standardized the calendar for centuries to come. This was called the *Julian calendar.*

Over time, however, the small errors in Caesar's calculation compounded. That's why Pope

Gregory XIII commissioned the *Gregorian calendar,* used in most of the world today. Some countries converted in 1582, when the calendar was first developed; some converted later; other still haven't changed.

Gregorian and Julian aren't the only types of calendars. The Hebrew year, the Islamic year, and many other calendars are used in different parts of the world and among different people.

You can convert Gregorian dates to other calendars, including the Hebrew calendar, the Islamic calendar, and even the Mayan calendar by visiting the Fourmilab Calendar Converter at http://www.fourmilab.ch/documents/calendar/.

A 50-year brass perpetual calendar.

Copyright, Credit, and Contact

Follow Us

Our blog Dobson's Improbable History features short articles on events and people associated with each day, and updates several times each week. Get the latest on Twitter @SidewiseThinker.

Contact Us

Find an error or a format problem? Want information about the series, about us, or about when the volume for your special day might be available? Please email us at editor@timespinnerpress.com.

Sources and Art Credits

All art and photographs are either in the public domain or used under a Creative Commons license. Attribution is provided where requested by the copyright owner or when of historical significance, listed below.

- The cover photograph of a stained glass window dedicated to Saint Patrick at the Church of the Assumption, Our Lady's Island, County Wexford, Ireland, was taken in 2010 by Andreas F. Borchert. It is used here under the Creative Commons Attribution-Share Alike 3.0 Germany license.

- The photograph of the statue of Saint Patrick outside St. John's Seminary in Brighton, Massachusetts, was taken by John Stephen Dwyer and is used here under the Creative Commons Attribution-Share Alike 3.0 Unported license.

- The engraving of the British evacuating Boston is from the Library of Congress Prints and Photographs Division. It is in the public domain because its copyright has expired.

- *Caricature of King Victor Emmanuel II* by Thomas Nast is in the collection of the Brooklyn Museum, New York. It is in the public domain because its copyright has expired.

- The photograph of the memorial in former German-Nazi extermination camp in Belzec is by Lysy, and is used here under the Creative Commons Attribution-Share Alike 3.0 Unported license.

- The photograph of the collapsed Ludendorff Bridge at Remagen is in the public domain because it was taken by an employee of the United States government as part of that person's official duties. The original is in the Franklin D. Roosevelt Library and Museum.

- The photograph of the DSV *Alvin* is in the public domain because it was taken by an employee of the United States government as part of that person's official duties.

- The 1973 photograph of Golda Meir was a work for hire by a U.S. News & World Report photographer, and is part of a collection donated to the Library of Congress. Per the deed of gift, all rights in this photograph were dedicated to the public.

- The photograph of Rob Lowe was taken by the U.S. Navy and as a work of the Federal government is in the public domain.

- The photograph of Gary Sinese at the National Press Club was taken by Marine Lance Cpl. Bryan G. Carfrey and is in the public domain as a work of the U.S. government.

- The photo of Brigitte Helm is from the "Die bunte Welt des Films" series published by Haus Bergmann tobacco company in 1934, and is in the public domain according to the Berne convention Article 7.

- The illustration of Polly from Bret Harte's *The Queen of the Pirate Isle*, created by Kate Greenaway, is in the public domain because its copyright has expired.

- The photograph of Rudolf Nureyev is by Hugo Cambiasso, and is used here under the Creative Commons Attribution 3.0 Unported license.

- The photograph of John Sebastian performing in concert in August 1970 is by Hugh Shirley Candyside, and is used here under the Creative Commons Attribution-Share Alike 2.0 Generic license.

- The 1947 photograph of Nat King Cole is by William P. Gottlieb and is part of the William P. Gottlieb Collection at the Library of Congress Music Division. Per wishes of Gottlieb, the photographs in the collection are in the public domain.

- The screenshot of George Harrison and Pattie Boyd from *A Hard Day's Night* is taken from a copyrighted film. It is used here under the "Fair Use" provision of the copyright code. The image is of a lower resolution than the original photograph (copies made from it will be of inferior quality). The photo is being used for informational purposes only, and its use is not believed to detract from the original in any way. No free alternative is known to be available, and one of the subjects is deceased.

- The photograph of the Terra Nova Expedition is in the public domain because its copyright has expired.

- The 1965 photograph of Bayard Rustin was taken by Stanley Wolfson for the New York *World-Telegram and Sun*. It is part of a collection donated by the *World-Telegram and Sun* to the Library of Congress Prints and Photographs Division, and per deed of gift from the donor is in the public domain.

- The photograph of astronaut Jim Irwin is in the public domain as a work created by NASA.

- The photograph of Olympian Ralph Rose is in the public domain because its copyright has expired.

- The screenshot of Helen Hayes from the trailer for the 1934 film *What Every Woman Knows* is in the public domain because it was published between 1923 and 1977 without a copyright notice.

- The photograph of the courtyard of the Salk Institute for Biological Studies in San Diego, California, was taken by "TheNose" and is used here under the Creative Commons Attribution-Share Alike 2.0 Generic license.

- The wood engraving of Juraj Jánošík is by Władysław

Skoczylas. It is in the public domain because its copyright has expired.

- The bust of Roman emperor Marcus Aurelius is from the Spanish Royal Collection, located in the Prado Museum. It was taken by Luis Garciá in 2006. It is used here under the Creative Commons Attribution-Share Alike 2.0 Generic license.

- The 1921 photograph of Irène Joliot-Curie was taken by James Stokley and is in the collection of the Smithsonian Institution. No known copyright restrictions on this photograph exist.

- The image of François de La Rochefoucauld is in the public domain because its copyright has expired.

- The illustration of the month of March used on the back cover and in the interior is from the French Gothic illuminated manuscript *Les Très Riches Heures du duc de Berry* by the Limbourg Brothers, Jean Colombe, and an intermediate painter whose name is lost to history. It is in the public domain because its copyright has expired.

- The photograph of aquamarine has been released into the public domain.

- The photograph of daffodils is by Myrabella, and is licensed under the Creative Commons Attribution-Share Alike 3.0 Unported license.

- The 1917 Women's Suffrage demonstration comes from the Library of Congress, Prints and Photographs Division, LC-USZ62-31799 DLC, and is in the public domain because its copyright has expired.

- The 50-year perpetual calendar photograph is in the public domain.

The month of March, from the illuminated manuscript *Les Très Riches Heures du duc de Berry*

Timespinner
Press

www.ingramcontent.com/pod-product-compliance
Lightning Source LLC
Chambersburg PA
CBHW050426290526
45786CB00003B/1418